a LEISURE-PLAN book in c

roses for every garden

F. C. H. WITCHELL

contents

Leisure-Plan books in colour are for pleasure and better living — the special kind of pleasure which comes from success with a rewarding hobby or pastime.

Authoritative, lively, packed with up-to-date information, these books can be built into a library for the whole family.

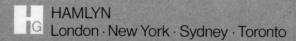

HAMLYN
London · New York · Sydney · Toronto

Front cover: City of Belfast   Back cover: King's Ransom

roses in the garden

The objectives of this book are simple and relatively limited. It does not set out to be a stuffy, all-embracing treatise on the genus *Rosa*. It seeks only to show how ordinary people like you and me and the man next door, using easy modern techniques, can grow lots of beautiful high-quality roses without the expenditure of too much time, money, tears or sweat.

The rose family is one of extraordinary versatility with such a wide range of attractions that it well deserves the title often bestowed upon it, 'the queen of flowers'. Just consider for a moment some of the things it can offer: a beautiful display of colour in the garden for up to five months of the year, many different kinds and forms of flower, an exceptional range of types and sizes of plant from 6 in. miniatures to great rampant climbers, lovely cut blooms to beautify the home and, very often, with a delightful perfume. Quite an impressive catalogue of virtues; yet in return for all this the rose demands so little. It is very easy to grow, asking for the application of only a little commonsense and a few occasional attentions.

Since the rose is a form of garden furnishing and decoration – and a relatively permanent one at that, because good plants can grow and flower bounteously for many years – it is wise to spend a little time planning how and where to use the various sorts most effectively, before rushing out to buy and plant rose bushes.

So let us begin by examining some of the different kinds of roses that are freely available today, and see if we can generate some ideas about how to use them to produce pleasing and satisfying effects. Except for those specifically stated to do otherwise, you can take it that they will all flower more or less continuously right through the summer and, often, well into the autumn too. You will be able to buy scented varieties in every group except, perhaps, the polyantha.

Starting at the bottom of the measurement scale with the babies of the family, we have what you will find described in rose growers' catalogues as the miniature roses. These are tiny bush roses which vary in height from 6 to about 15 in. with a spread of perhaps an inch or two more. They can be bought in white, yellow and most shades of pink, salmon and red. They make lovely permanent edging plants, can be used to fill small beds, as features in a rockery and even for planting in tubs, troughs and window boxes.

Next in size is a group called the polyantha roses. They grow from 1 to 2 ft. tall and usually spread as much or a little more. The flowers, which come in large clusters, are quite small, generally about 1 in. across. These can be had in the same range of colours as the miniature

*For the convenience of the reader the colour illustrations of rose varieties are placed in alphabetical order, with minor variations.

Anna Wheatcroft, with its large, light vermilion flowers, is a good garden floribunda rose, and is popular for exhibition. Trial Ground Certificate

David
Austen Rose
Prairie Princess
"Pink"

roses. Polyantha varieties are very useful for small rose beds or borders grown on their own or for decorating the front of large beds.

The middle of the size range is occupied by the two most popular kinds of bush rose of our time. These are the floribundas and the hybrid teas. Here we find varieties of all sizes from 2 to over 4 ft. tall with flowers in almost every colour except green or blue.

Floribunda roses produce their flowers in quite large trusses and make bold displays of colour in the garden. There is a wide range of flower forms: single, semi-double, fully double, rosette and what most people recognise as the 'real' rose shape, the high-centred hybrid tea form. The flowers vary in size from about $1\frac{1}{2}$ to nearly 4 in. across when fully open.

The hybrid tea roses produce their flowers either one to a stem or in smallish clusters, hence their popularity as cut flowers for the house and for flower arrangements. In most varieties the blooms possess the aforesaid 'real rose' shape and are larger than the floribundas, the flowers opening up to as much as 5 in. across.

These two groups of tough and hardy roses, because of their variety and versatility, have a number of uses. They make, for example, colourful flower beds and borders and can be used for hedges and for screening unsightly objects from view.

Quite a few floribunda and hybrid tea varieties can be bought as 'standards', that is, bushes growing on top of $3\frac{1}{2}$ ft. stems. These make interesting feature plants if strategically placed in a bed or border of bush roses.

Growing from 2 ft. to much bigger even than the hybrid teas, we come to a large selection of species and hybrids often lumped together under the heading of 'old fashioned' or shrub roses. Some varieties flower once only in the season – watch this point when choosing – and some produce brightly coloured seed-pods (called hips) after the flowers have faded.

(Top)
Tiny rose heads are part of the novelty of miniature roses. Here a selection of varieties has been arranged to illustrate the variation in the size and form of the blooms

(Bottom)
A hedge of floribunda Queen Elizabeth makes a colourful and practical addition to the garden

(Top)
Hybrid tea Ena Harkness has been budded on to a 3½ ft. briar stock stem to form a standard rose

(Bottom)
An example of a climbing rose used as a 'pillar', that is, trained on a single pole. The variety is Chaplin's Pink Climber

(Top)
Many ramblers, like **New Dawn** illustrated here, can be trained into an attractive low-growing hedge

(Bottom)
An unsightly garage or garden shed can be masked simply with a climber or rambler rose. Here Zépherine Drouhin has been used, together with the floribunda, Goldilocks

The Queen Mary's Garden in Regent's Park is a good place to see roses growing. Here are some of the beds of hybrid tea roses

Several have beautiful foliage that is a delight to the flower arranger. Many of them want a lot of room to grow in and so are useful in a border of mixed shrubs or grown as single specimen bushes.

Biggest of all are the climbers and ramblers. They make shoots from 6 to 20 ft. long according to variety. Some climbers flower more or less all through the summer, some once only. All those classed as ramblers flower just once – usually three to four weeks sees the best of the display. As a generalisation, climbers tend to make a more or less permanent framework of growth while the ramblers grow long new shoots one year which flower in the next summer and are then discarded, by cutting them away. One can visualise both these roses being trained on fences, trellises or over arches or pergolas. For house walls use climbers, not ramblers.

There are several commonsense points to remember about planning and siting roses in the garden. Keep low growers in front of tall ones, and put dark colours in front of light ones so that you get maximum effect. Bear in mind safety and utility, too. Roses have thorns which scratch and hurt, so do not plant bushes too close to paths, drives or doorways. Remember that windows must be cleaned and houses painted, so leave room for people to work and ladders to rest.

Finally, roses are easy to grow but even roses will be unhappy if planted in impossible positions. Places to avoid are those which do not get any sun or rain, or are in draught tunnels, directly under overhanging trees where they will be in the shade and where rain will drop from the trees onto the roses, or in close competition with some greedy monster of a plant like a privet hedge. These are all elementary points but are much better considered and planned for first than painfully discovered later, when your roses fail to thrive and a solution has to be found!

A good selection of floribunda roses can be seen in the Princess Mary Rose Borders in the Royal National Rose Society's gardens at St Albans

(Top)
This rose bed is sited in a good sunny position, open on all sides except to the north

(Bottom)
Roses will not flourish when planted in the positions shown here; they will be shaded by both the hedge and trees and the overhanging trees will drip rain onto the blooms. Tree, hedge and rose roots will all have to forage for food and moisture in the same limited area

(Top)
This is an almost impossible position for roses to grow successfully as they will get no sun or rain

(Bottom)
This is not an ideal planting area as the fence cuts off the western sun and rain, making the back of the bed very dry. The overhanging tree will create shade, keep off the rain which will drip from the tree leaves to the flowers

choosing your roses

Having decided how and where we want to use roses in the garden, the next step is to choose the varieties that will best fit the places selected and give us the most joy. And this is where we need to have some inside knowledge because it is possible to make some bad mistakes.

One way you can select your roses is to send for a glossy rose catalogue, look at the coloured pictures, read the glowing descriptions, make your choice, send off the order form and hope for the best. But there are snags. Even modern printing technology, advanced though it may be, is often defeated by nature's artfully delicate tints and shades, with the result that some of the colour plates in even the best catalogues may be very misleading. Also, although leading nurserymen do their best to be honest with their catalogue descriptions of varieties, they may not know or may omit to mention that a specific variety absolutely detests your particular district or soil and will not grow well in it, or is not very resistant to disease.

It is by far the best bet to choose your roses by going and seeing them actually growing and flowering, so that you can be sure that you are really going to like what you buy. You can do this by visiting a good nursery to see the plants in bloom during the summer. Preferably, go to two or three nurseries and compare the size and quality of the plants growing in them, and go more than once during the season, say, in July, August and September, as some roses may look their best at one time and not so good at others. Some varieties dislike wet weather and some are liable to get a touch of mildew or black spot late in the summer. If you see a variety three times in three different months and if it appeals to you every time, that one is for you.

Before visiting a nursery check if it has a permanent display garden where you can see established bushes growing. The point is that if you see only the young bushes in the nursery beds, you may have difficulty in judging just how big the bushes will become after they have been growing in your own garden for several years. This is particularly true of the larger-growing floribundas, hybrid teas, shrubs, climbers and ramblers.

Some of the most progressive and efficient rose nurseries provide large car parks, even picnic areas, to make it easy and pleasant for you to go to spend happy afternoons quietly browsing among the roses and making your choice at leisure.

Other places to see established trees growing include the lovely gardens maintained by the Royal National Rose Society at St. Albans (but you must be a member – it is well worth joining or persuading a member to take you); the special rose display gardens in Regent's Park, London; Syon Park, Middlesex; The Northern Horticultural Society's Gardens at

Harlow Car, Harrogate; Roath Park, Cardiff; Saughton Park, Edinburgh; Vivary Park, Taunton; and other public parks which have large displays of roses.

It is also a good idea to seek out one or two expert amateur rosarians in your district. They are usually friendly people who will be delighted to give a beginner information and advice. Your local horticultural society will probably introduce you to them.

When choosing roses, there are a couple of points about which it is wise to get confirmation before you actually buy the plants. Roses vary in their resistance to three diseases. These are mildew, black spot and rust. Mildew is easy to spot. When looking at roses in August and September, you may see a whitish coating on the young leaves and on the flower buds and stalks. That is mildew. It is not usually a dangerous disease; it just spoils the appearance of the bushes. But if you do not like it, then avoid those varieties on which you see it.

Black spot attacks roses grown only in clean-air districts. If you live in such a district, look in September for dark-coloured spots on the lower leaves and look, too, for trees from which black spot has caused the leaves to fall. Check with your nurseryman or a local expert about the liability of your chosen varieties to contract the disease. There are not too many varieties with a serious weakness for black spot, but it could be your misfortune to have

(Top)
Apricot Nectar is one of the relatively few apricot coloured roses. It is a floribunda whose flowers are above average in size. Certificate of Merit
(Bottom)
Arthur Bell has a lovely golden-yellow colour which fades a little as the flowers open. An unusually fragrant floribunda rose. Certificate of Merit

chosen one of those that are susceptible to it.

Rust is a relatively rare disease which does not occur on many varieties or in every district, but it can be a killer. It is a disease that the uninitiated are unlikely to spot, so be wise and check before you order that the varieties you choose are not liable to contract it.

At the other extreme, if you live in a heavily built-up industrial area with a dirty atmosphere, make your choice from the tough, strong-growing varieties which can put up with local conditions. Again, check with the nurseryman.

Lastly, then, is the choice of whether to order trees from a nursery for autumn planting, or to buy trees in containers from a garden centre, which can be planted at any time of the year. Personally, I prefer the former, but the container-grown trees do have their own appeal. Provided you have the ground properly prepared for these bushes, and can be assured that the trees have actually been grown in their containers – and not just dug up and dumped in them a few weeks earlier – there is no reason why this sort of 'instant gardening' should not be successful.

My next chapter on roses for special purposes has been compiled with the object of helping you make an interesting choice, but in rose growing as in every other aspect of decorative gardening it must be personal preferences which count for most.

roses with special qualities

In addition to carrying out their task of giving you much pleasure and satisfaction by beautifying your garden effectively, you may require some special qualities of the roses you wish to grow. Qualities, for example, of being specially good for cutting for the house or having above-average fragrance. Obviously, not all roses can boast all of the qualities, so it is the purpose of this chapter to examine some of the special qualities frequently desired, and to indicate just a few of the varieties which possess them. But please regard the lists of names given later merely as pointers as to where to start looking – there is really no substitute for seeing roses growing and being sure you will like them before making the final decision to buy.

Many of the varieties named in this chapter are displayed in the captioned colour plates which illustrate this book, but those not illustrated are described in Chapter 13.

Roses for cutting
It is a very disappointing experience to cut an armful of beautiful buds to decorate the home and then discover that, within twenty-four hours, those lovely tight buds have flown open and the effect of the carefully arranged bowl is largely lost. Fortunately, there are some varieties that can be relied upon to last for several days in water if treated properly. Never cut roses in the heat of the day. Cut young blooms on which the outer petals are just starting to open, and do this in the cool of early morning or late evening. Plunge them up to their necks in fresh water – preferably containing one of the cut flower preservatives now on the market – and keep them in a cool place either for a few hours or overnight. Do your arrangement later in the day or in the morning – again using the preservative. Always use a scrupulously clean container for the arrangement if you want your roses to last well, and do not forget to keep the water level well topped up.

The following varieties have a good reputation for lasting reasonably well in water. In general, the hybrid teas last longer than the floribundas.

Hybrid Teas
Gavotte, Grandpa Dickson, Lady Seton, Mischief, Miss Ireland, Mojave, Montezuma, Princess, Red Devil, Rose Gaujard, Silver Lining, Wendy Cussons

Floribundas
Daily Sketch, Elizabeth of Glamis, Iceberg, Lilli Marlene, Paddy McGredy, Plentiful, Queen Elizabeth, Rosemary Rose

Roses for floral art
The qualities required of a rose for floral art work are somewhat more exacting than those

required of a rose for home display. They include beauty of form, a light and elegant appearance, fresh and bright colour, a good length of stem and fresh, attractive foliage. Clearly, if faced with the problems of creating arrangements that may have to remain in situ for several days – as happens at festivals and with church decoration – you will try to select varieties that will hold their form in water for the required length of time. In many floral art shows, however, the arrangements are exhibited for one day only and, if these are the circumstances, there is less need for the roses to have such long-lasting qualities.

Modern roses which are popular for floral art work include:

Hybrid Teas
Blue Moon, First Love, Fragrant Cloud, Grand'mère Jenny, Lady Seton, Message, Mischief, Mojave, Montezuma, President Herbert Hoover (in autumn), Rose Gaujard, Super Star, Sutter's Gold, Uncle Walter, Virgo, Wendy Cussons, Youki San

Floribundas
Cécile Brunner, Chanelle, Dorothy Wheatcroft, Elizabeth of Glamis, Iceberg, Plentiful, Queen Elizabeth, Rosemary Rose

Roses to win at your local show
There are few better tests of a gardener's skill than competing in a local show. Success here is confirmation that you are growing your roses to a satisfactory standard and, anyway, exhibiting is a lot of fun. To win a prize at a show a rose needs to be of perfect form; fresh and bright in colour; unmarked by rain, pest or disease; of good size and substance and be supported by a good stem with fine clean and bright undamaged leaves.

When cutting roses for exhibition, use the same techniques as for cutting for the home,

but study your own particular varieties. See how long it takes them to open from the bud to the perfect form state. Then ascertain from the show schedule the time of the day at which the exhibits are to be judged and, with your knowledge of the particular traits of the roses you grow, decide when and at what stage of development to cut them.

The following are a few of the roses which combine both the qualities of being good garden roses and the capability to produce exhibition blooms with little encouragement.

Hybrid Teas
Fragrant Cloud, Gavotte, Grandpa Dickson, Isabel de Ortiz, Pink Favourite, Princess, Red Devil, Red Lion, Royal Highness, Stella, Super Star, Wendy Cussons

Floribundas
Alain, Anna Wheatcroft, Elizabeth of Glamis, Europeana, Iceberg, Orangeade, Pink Parfait, Queen Elizabeth

Roses for fragrance
Some people are quite content to have a bright and attractive display of balanced colour groupings in their gardens without serious concern about fragrance. And, let us frankly admit, there are some of us whose noses are very inefficient at detecting even the most prominent of smells. Many gardeners, however, will feel the need to have around them roses that are both delightful to look at and sweetly and strongly perfumed.

The list which follows consists only of modern garden roses which fulfil both purposes but, if perfume is all important to you, even at the expense of continuous flowering, it would be useful to examine the possibilities of some of the species and 'old fashioned' roses, many of which are exquisitely perfumed.

Casino is a lovely yellow climber which you can grow equally well on a pillar, wall or fence. Gold Medal

Hybrid Teas
Blue Moon, Diorama, Duke of Windsor, Ernest H. Morse, Fragrant Cloud, Lady Seton, Prima Ballerina, Princess Paola, Red Devil

Floribundas
Apricot Nectar, Charm of Paris, Elizabeth of Glamis, Lucky Charm, Scented Air

Rain-resistant roses

Most of us accept that the sort of cold and wet spells with which our British summers are usually so freely interspersed will spoil, for a time, the brightness of our gardens. But some gardeners may be prepared to restrict their plantings to a very limited number of varieties of roses provided that they can be reasonably assured that a spell of bad weather will not ruin the display of colour completely.

To some extent the natural ability of a variety to tolerate rain can be helped or handicapped by the situation in which it is planted in the garden. Planted in a warm sunny position where there is a good circulation of air (but not a whistling draught) so that the bushes can dry off quickly, they will put up their best performance. But when they are planted in shady places, near trees or dense shrubberies where the atmosphere tends to remain cold and damp, they will not do so well.

The rose that never marks in really bad weather, wherever it is planted, has yet to be bred, but those listed below display above-average tolerance of our uncertain climate.

Hybrid Teas
Ernest H. Morse, Fragrant Cloud, Gail Borden, Grandpa Dickson, Mischief, Piccadilly, Pink Favourite, Rose Gaujard, Stella, Super Star, Wendy Cussons

Floribundas
Allgold, City of Belfast, Elizabeth of Glamis,

(*Top*)
Blue Moon is probably the best of the 'blue' hybrid tea roses so far produced. It has the merit of being quite strongly perfumed. **Certificate of Merit**

(*Bottom*)
Chicago Peace, a hybrid tea rose, is a 'sport' from Peace. The attractive flowers are large and of good form. It is a very strong grower with glossy leathery foliage

(*Top*)
Chinatown grows to massive proportions which makes it useful for hedging. **Gold Medal**

(*Bottom*)
City of Leeds is a really attractive rich salmon floribunda with quite large flowers. **Gold Medal**

Floribundas continued
Evelyn Fison, Iceberg, Korona, Lilli Marlene, Orangeade, Paprika, Queen Elizabeth, Red Favourite, Sarabande

Roses for the small garden
Many new gardens in this country are very small indeed as the world is becoming more densely populated, and the dwellings in which we live are tending to be built closer and closer together.

Provided, however, that plenty of sun and life-giving rain can get to a small garden and the soil is well drained, there is no reason why any tiny garden on fair soil should not grow a wide selection of good roses. But the owner will probably not be satisfied to fill it with a few strong-growing bushes which, in any case, will crowd it and seem out of proportion. For such a garden there are the miniatures and the dwarf polyanthas; but there are quite a few hybrid teas and floribunda roses too, that do not grow more than a couple of feet high and would be perfectly suitable. Here are a few fine roses from each class.

Miniatures
Baby Masquerade, Colibre, Coralin, Perla d' Alcanada, Pour Toi, Rosina, Scarlet Gem, Sweet Fairy

Dwarf Polyanthas
Baby Faurax, Cameo, Coral Cluster, Ellen Poulsen, Miss Edith Cavell, Paul Crampel

Hybrid Teas
Champs Elysées, Cleopatra, Colour Wonder, Doreen, Fritz Thiedemann, Mme Louis Laperrière, Princess, Wisbech Gold

Floribundas
Africa Star, Allgold, Athlone, Bobbie Lucas, Escapade, Golden Slippers, Jan Spek, Lilli Marlene, Marlena, Orange Sensation

Floribundas continued
Plentiful, Red Favourite, Rosemary Rose, Sarabande, Zambra

Roses for hedges
Where there is sufficient space there is no doubt that a rose hedge can be a very attractive feature of a garden. Though it offers little privacy when in its leafless state during the winter months, it may be considered to compensate for that with a long display of glorious colour during most of the summer and autumn.

The qualities required of a rose that is to be used for hedging include strength and a reasonable uprightness of growth, hardiness, lots of flowers, a long flowering season, good foliage and a fair degree of disease resistance. It is best to avoid the 'twiggy' growers and those with masses of vicious, close packed thorns – they are the very devil to prune as you can imagine.

It is usually considered desirable to plant the bushes in a single row and to plant them fairly closely together – 18 to 24 inches apart is about right for most of the recommended hedging varieties. Just because it is a hedge and not a display bed in the garden, do not neglect the feeding and watering. This care of the roses is just as important as the selection of the variety to ensure a satisfactory and long-lived hedge.

These are suitable roses for the purpose:

Hybrid Teas
Buccaneer, Peace, Rose Gaujard, Uncle Walter

Floribundas
Chinatown, Dorothy Wheatcroft, Frensham, Queen Elizabeth, Scarlet Queen Elizabeth

Shrub Roses
Bonn, Fred Loads, Heidelberg, Kassel, Lady Sonia

Roses for standards

Standard roses are those that are budded at the top of a tall briar stem, usually at a point about three-and-a-half feet above ground level. They are useful as 'dot' plants in a large bed or border, providing interesting height variations. Because of the habit of growth or other reasons, not all varieties make satisfactory standard trees. Some that are usually successful are:

Hybrid Teas
Champs Elysées, Ena Harkness, Fragrant Cloud, King's Ransom, Mischief, Piccadilly, Super Star, Wendy Cussons

Floribundas
Dearest, Elizabeth of Glamis, Evelyn Fison, Gold Marie, Orangeade, Paprika, Red Dandy

Roses that climb

'Climbing' roses vary considerably in their habits of growth, in their likes and dislikes of situations and in their freedom and continuity of flowering. Some flower for a short period only in the summer, some dislike north or east aspects, some – especially the ramblers – get smothered in mildew in no time at all. Here are a few of the safer varieties that a beginner may find interesting and attractive:

Altissimo, Casino, Copenhagen, Danse du Feu, Dortmund, Golden Showers, Hamburger Phoenix, Handel, Parkdirektor Riggers, Pink Perpetue, Ritter von Barmstede, Royal Gold, Schoolgirl, New Dawn, Zéphirine Drouhin

(Above right)
An arrangement of five hybrid tea roses with accompanying foliage

(Right)
A prizewinning exhibit staged by the author at a Royal National Rose Show

(Top)
The orange-yellow blooms of Copper Pot are in striking contrast to the dark green foliage of this upright-growing floribunda. Trial Ground Certificate

(Bottom)
Danse du Feu is an average-sized climber that looks attractive on a pillar, wall or fence. Certificate of Merit

(Top)
Dorothy Peach is a hybrid tea which can give some really beautiful blooms and is very free with its flowers, especially in late summer. It may need protection from black spot. Gold Medal

(Bottom)
Dorothy Wheatcroft is a good floribunda which grows very big and shrubby, and flowers freely. Gold Medal

(*Top*)
Elizabeth of Glamis is a very beautiful floribunda combining the virtues of delightful colour, elegant form and fragrance. President's International Trophy

(*Bottom*)
Ena Harkness is a very popular crimson-scarlet hybrid tea rose of very elegant form, with moderate fragrance. It has a tendency to hang its head unless well fed and watered. Gold Medal

(*Top*)
The very fragrant hybrid tea rose Duke of Windsor is of good form and is a bright, attractive orange-vermilion colour. Certificate of Merit

(*Bottom*)
Ernest H. Morse, the hybrid tea rose, has glorious perfume demonstrating that the 'old rose fragrance' has not been lost in modern varieties. Gold Medal

preparing to plant roses

Roses, in their needs, have much in common with children. Given a nice comfortable bed in good healthy conditions and some nourishing food at regular intervals, they will thrive, and reward you with masses of blooms.

In the first chapter we discussed the siting of roses in the garden and noted some impossible positions where we should not ask them to try to grow. There are several other conditions rose bushes will not like, either, such as waterlogged ground, poor, starved ground lacking in nutrients, extremely acid or alkaline soil, or a spot without sufficient depth of soil for their roots to wander and forage. Subject to these provisos, roses will grow well in any soil from light sandy loam to heavy clay. The old wives' tale that rose trees grow well only in clay soil is nonsense.

Now, the beginner's first problem is how to know whether his soil is one in which roses will grow well and, if not, how to improve it. For a start, look at what is growing there now. If the ground grows a good healthy crop of weeds, vegetables or herbaceous flowers, there is probably nothing fundamentally wrong with it. But it might be a little too acid or alkaline for perfect blooms and this is very easy to discover. Just buy a soil testing outfit – some brands cost very little – that shows on a colour scale whether your soil provides the perfect conditions for growing good roses.

If an ordinary loam or clay soil passes the test and seems right for planting the bushes, prepare the bed really well for the roses. Remember that they are going to be there for a very long time, so you might as well take a little trouble to do the job properly.

My own method is to clear off the weeds or whatever vegetation is growing there and spread a good 2 in. thick dressing of fine peat all over the bed. Then take a full-size garden fork and, thrusting it in to its full depth, fork over the ground really thoroughly until the peat is well mixed in and all the lumps of soil are broken down into crumbs. It is seldom, if ever, necessary to dig deeper than this. This treatment of loosening the soil will ensure that there is an easy root run for the new trees and the peat will improve the texture of the soil. The addition of plant foods we will leave until after the trees have been planted.

This soil preparation – the only hard work in growing roses – must be completed well before the trees are planted because the soil has been really loosened up and it needs time to settle a little. About a month is long enough for a light soil, but three months should be best allowed for heavy clay.

At this point I must add that, if you happen to read the rest of this chapter before you check your soil, do not let it terrify you. Ninety per cent of people will find that their soil is already right for roses. But I must go on to tell you how to cope just in case you should be one of the unfortunate 10% with unsuitable soil.

Now, supposing the soil test indicates that the soil is too acid? In that case the treatment is the same as described before for preparing the soil except for the need to add a dressing of lime to reduce the acidity. The colour test should indicate how much lime to use. For a soil which already contains a lot of peat, then omit the peat top dressing. Be careful not to overdo the liming – you can always put on some more, but an excess of lime is nothing like as easy to correct.

What do you do if the soil test shows the soil to be too alkaline? For a soil only slightly on the wrong side of neutral, use more peat – which tends to be very slightly acid – in the preparatory dressing and do not use any lime or alkaline fertilisers for some years to come. But if the topsoil is obviously very alkaline indeed, there is no reliable method of correcting the balance quickly. You will be risking the health of your rose bushes by planting them in soil like this. The reason why very alkaline soil is bad for roses is that it denies them iron in their diet – which, like us, they need – and they will suffer from yellowing of the leaves (called lime-induced chlorosis) in consequence. You can, if you are very keen and can afford the expense, import some good soil into the garden and spread it at least 1 ft. deep on top of the existing ground where the roses are to grow. Thus you will make these beds higher than the rest of the ground and keep the rose roots above the alkaline soil.

If you do decide to take the risk of planting roses in very alkaline soil, you will need to spray them regularly every summer with a substance called Sequestrene – which is, in effect, a medicinal way of giving them the iron they need – but this can be quite an expensive business.

Let us now turn to the problems of ground which is right for roses except for becoming waterlogged whenever a lot of rain falls. This

(Top)
A dressing of hydrated lime being applied to a rose bed to reduce acidity, which a soil test has shown to be excessive

(Bottom)
One of several soil testing outfits which are freely available in gardening shops and centres

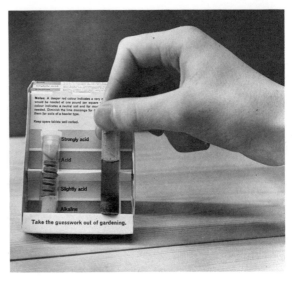

is easy to correct. It is merely a matter of raising the level of the bed sufficiently to keep the rose roots out of the water. Soil can be taken from somewhere else in the garden for the purpose. One way of doing this is to make a 12 in. to 18 in. deep cinder path round the bed, using the excavated soil to raise the level of the bed. This method also has the effect of lessening the liability to waterlogging, because the deep cinder path tends to act as a sump into which the water drains.

To remedy a case where there are only a few inches of soil lying on top of, for example, solid rock, the solution is, once again, to obtain soil from somewhere else to build up the rose bed until there is 12 in. or more of good earth on top of the rock.

One problem that most of us have to face sooner or later is that of clearing out and replanting an old rose bed. If it has grown roses for no longer than five years, all you need to do is dig up the old trees, getting out all the roots you can find, and then going through the basic soil preparation routine I described earlier – a dressing of fine peat and a good forking over.

But a bed which has grown roses for longer than five years must be getting what is called 'rose sick', and new roses planted in it are likely to fail. To solve this problem you must change the soil, not necessarily that of the whole bed but certainly where the new roses are to be planted. The method of doing this is to mark out the positions for the new trees and, at each position, dig out and take away an 18 in. cube of soil. Exchange this for some fresh soil – that has not recently grown roses – from another part of the garden and you are ready to replant the bed.

You are now finished with the soil preparation and have only two other jobs to do before planting your roses. One is to mark out the planting positions in the beds with canes or sticks. In spacing out the bushes you must allow for their subsequent growth to maturity. As a general and rather rough guide, miniatures may be planted 9 in. to 15 in. apart according to their height and spread; polyanthas, 15 in. to 24 in. apart; floribundas and hybrid teas, 2 ft. to 3 ft. apart and shrubs, 3 ft. to 6 ft. apart. Climbers and ramblers will want to be able to spread sideways from 8 ft. to 20 ft. Check with your nurseryman on the vigour of the varieties you propose to order and space them out accordingly.

The second and last job is to prepare the supports for your roses. Put in stakes to support standard trees, erect your arches, pergolas or trellises for your climbers and ramblers and, if you are going to put climbers on a wall, fix the straining wires, battens or whatever you intend to attach the rose stems to. Incidentally, do not use creosote as a wood preservative for anything you will use to support roses, as it does them no good. Use instead one of the proprietary products designed for the purpose. It is important to get all these preparations over before the roses are planted. These simple jobs are made unnecessarily hard and messy if they are done afterwards, apart from the fact that you will probably injure those beautiful trees in the process.

(*Top left*)
Goldgleam's deep yellow floribunda flowers contrast well with its small, dark green foliage. Trial Ground Certificate

(*Bottom left*)
The golden-yellow blooms of Golden Showers fade as they age. This climber can also be grown as a large shrub

(*Top right*)
Fred Loads is a beautiful shrub rose with large single flowers which are slightly perfumed. It has good, strong, upright growth. Certificate of Merit

(*Bottom right*)
Evelyn Fison's vivid red colouring always stands out in a garden display. A very good and popular floribunda. Gold Medal

planting roses

It is traditionally accepted that the best times to plant roses – except those bought in containers from a garden centre, and therefore planted at almost any time – are autumn and spring. Within these seasons, I prefer the month of November for autumn planting and March for spring planting.

Let us deal firstly with roses that arrive from a nursery. When the parcel is delivered, open it as soon as possible and examine the roses to see that they are in good condition and are, in fact, the varieties ordered. The tops of the bushes may or may not have been trimmed for easier packing. If the trees are climbers or ramblers, leave them as they are, but if they are any other kind, prune them ready for planting. It is much easier to prune before planting because the trees are easier to work on if you can hold them in your hand, turn them this way and that, and generally see much better what you are doing. The pruning process is quite simple: for floribundas, hybrid teas and shrubs, first cut off any leaves still on the trees, cut off broken and very thin twigs and cut away any bits of root that are damaged. What is left ought to be a sound bush with three or more good strong shoots of pencil thickness or greater. Shorten these to something like 8 to 10 in. in length. Make your cuts clean and straight across each shoot just $\frac{1}{4}$ in. above an eye. An 'eye' will be found where a set of leaves was growing and is the point from

(*Opposite page, left*)
Rose bushes newly arrived from the nursery have been out of the ground for some time and have lost moisture. The roots are given a twenty-four hour soaking and the bush is pruned before planting

(*Opposite page, right*)
The author digs the furrow ready to plant roses. Note that the marker canes are sticking out of the top of one side of the furrow

(*Below*)
Half of the bucket of peat and bonemeal planting mixture is spread on the side of the furrow from which the marker canes protrude

(*Bottom left*)
The bushes are put in position on the layer of peat and bonemeal. The author spreads the roots of the rose out along the furrow, and sets the bush so that the budding point is one inch below soil level

(*Top right*)
The roots are covered with the remaining half of the peat and bonemeal mixture and the soil is broken up and raked back into the furrow

(*Bottom right*)
The soil is trodden just enough to hold the bushes firmly. Stamping too hard could damage the roots

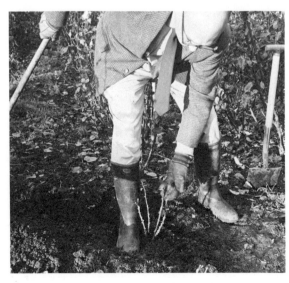

which new growth will be made in the spring.
Use high quality and very sharp secateurs to
ensure really good, clean cuts.

Pruning miniature and polyantha roses
follows the same pattern except that, being
smaller trees with thinner growth, the shoots
are cut back harder in proportion.

Next, all the roses, having been out of the
ground for some time during the packing and
transit period, want a drink. Give the roots a
good soaking in a bucket of water for not less
than twenty-four hours.

After this, the roses are ready for planting,
and you can get it completed at once unless the
ground is frozen or too sodden to work. If the
ground is unfit, put the bushes in a container
of damp fine peat and leave them in a cool
but frost-proof place until you can plant them.

When carrying out the planting operation
remember that the object of the exercise is to
bed the roses comfortably so that they will be
happy and grow strongly. Except if you
actually have a peat soil in your garden, make
up for each tree a planting mixture of a one-
gallon bucket of very damp (but not sodden)
fine grade peat into which you have mixed one
cupful of bonemeal.

A quick, easy and efficient way to plant roses
is as follows; the size of the hole described is
right for all kinds except the miniatures for
which a proportionately smaller hole is made
and less peat is used.

For each bush dig out a V-shaped furrow
18 in. long and about 10 in. deep beside the
marker cane you put in when preparing the
ground. When you have done this, the cane
should be sticking out from the top of one side
of the furrow and equidistant from both ends.
Spread half of the bucket of peat and bonemeal mixture on the sloping side of the furrow
next to the cane. Then lay the rose bush on
this beside the cane, so that the budding point
(where the shoots meet the root stem) is just
1 in. below normal soil level. Lay out the roots

(Below)
Fragrant Cloud is a hybrid tea rose that has gained considerable popularity for its combination of unusual colour, good shape and beautiful fragrance. President's International Trophy

(Top)
Gallant, a floribunda, has well shaped and quite large blooms. There is a little fragrance. Trial Ground Certificate

(Bottom)
Grand'mère Jenny, a hybrid tea rose of delightfully delicate colour tones and very elegant shape, can grow quite tall. The foliage is plentiful and glossy. Gold Medal

full stretch both ways along the furrow and cover them with the remainder of the peat and bonemeal. The bush's roots should now appear as the 'meat' in a sandwich of peat and bonemeal mixture. Now put the soil which you dug up back into the furrow, first breaking it up into small pieces if it is lumpy, and tread it down just enough to hold the rose firmly. But take care not to stamp the ground so hard as to hurt the roots. Lastly, take the cane out, rake the soil level and generally tidy up the planting area.

To plant a rose bought in a container from a garden centre, make a hole the same shape as the container but 3 in. or 4 in. wider and 2 in. deeper. The general idea is to plant the rose

bush without disturbing the soil round its roots. It will hold together best if it is quite damp but not really wet, so you might need to water the soil in the container. Next, line the bottom of the hole with a 2 in. layer of the peat and bonemeal planting mixture in the proportions already described. Cut the bottom out of the container, put the rose on the peat base, cut down the side of the container and lift it carefully away. Slip the rest of the peat and bonemeal between the soil ball and the sides of the hole, fill in with soil and firm it with your hands.

When you plant a standard rose tree, the procedure is the same as for a bush except that you will have no budding point to give a guide to depth of planting. If you can see the mark of the nursery soil level on the stem, plant to the same depth. If you cannot distinguish this mark, set the tree so that the topmost roots will be covered with 2 in. of soil when you have finished planting. Also, take care to plant the tree close beside the stake you put in earlier and secure the tree to the stake before you tidy up the ground. The modern sort of plastic tie is excellent for this job. Put the tie on a little below the top of the stem and leave it slightly loose because the tree may settle in the soil during the next few months.

After planting climbers or ramblers, spread the shoots out widely, bending them down a little if you can and tying them loosely to their supports. Never make ties so tight that the stems are strangled: this could kill the tree.

You will need, too, to make it a practice to check the ties about every six months, and adjust or replace ties that are tight, worn or broken. If you do not take this precaution, a gale may well tear down the tree and the rose would be lost. Regular inspection of the wooden stakes supporting standard trees and of arches or pergolas made of wood is also necessary because even treated wood must rot eventually and need replacing.

(*Top*)
The container-grown rose is pruned before being planted
(*Bottom*)
A hole for the rose bush is dug the same shape as the container but 4 in. wider and 2 in. deeper

(Top)
The bottom of the container is cut away, leaving the soil undisturbed around the roots. The rose is placed in the prepared hole on a bed of the planting mixture and the container is cut down the side and removed. The remaining planting mixture is then added round the soil ball

(Bottom)
The hole is filled with the dug-out soil

(Top)
The soil is firmed around the bush to complete the planting

(Bottom)
A standard rose tree is secured to its stake using an efficient modern tie. Note that the tie is set just below the top of the stem

feeding and watering roses

Having got your roses planted comfortably in their beds, you can begin to think about their diet. Plants, like us, need food and drink and need both a balanced diet and regular meals.

Spring may be regarded as breakfast time for roses when they respond to a feed, and early in April seems to suit them very well for this. There is no need for the beginner to rose growing to concern himself with mixing his own fertilisers. It is simpler and probably safer for him to buy a bag of one of the ready-prepared 'complete' fertilisers specially designed for roses – there are several good brands on the market. Personally, I prefer to use one that provides more potash than nitrogen and that also contains all the necessary 'trace' elements. There is no problem about this – just look at the small print on the bag before you buy; it should give the formula and state what trace elements are included.

Try to choose a calm day to apply the fertiliser – because it is usually of a fine texture – and sprinkle it on the ground all round, but not *on* the trees, in the quantities indicated in the instructions. Do not 'exceed the stated dose' – roses can get indigestion, too! You can gently hoe it into the surface if you are not

(Left)
Iceberg is the outstanding white floribunda rose. It flowers very freely on long, graceful shoots. It grows very tall but can bow down under a severe summer storm. Gold Medal

intending immediately to apply a 'mulch'.

The purpose of a mulch, which is simply a thin blanket of some sort of decayed animal or vegetable matter, is to conserve moisture in the soil and also to maintain humus. For this mulch, you can use horse or cow manure (if you can get it!), garden compost, spent hops (obtainable from a garden centre or nursery), grass cuttings or coarse grade peat. Note that you use fine grade peat for planting and *coarse* grade peat for mulching. Avoid pig or chicken manures on two counts – they may be too harsh for your trees, and the smell of them might well strain your friendship with your neighbours. Do not use grass cuttings from a lawn to which you have applied one of the hormone weedkillers within the course of the past three weeks.

Spread your chosen mulching material all over the whole rose bed, but not letting it actually touch the trees. Two to three inches thick is about right for horse or cow manure containing a lot of straw, half to one inch is thick enough for the other materials.

For an average garden display, that is all the food you need give to the older trees in your garden. If, however, you want to have really top class roses, give them some 'foliar' feeds (which we will describe later in this chapter) in May and June as well.

So far as water is concerned, well-established trees with good root systems can usually get all

(Top)
A complete rose fertiliser is spread around, but not on, rose bushes in the spring

(Bottom)
Using peat for a spring mulch on a rose bed

the water they need for themselves, but young, recently planted trees can't do this. You see, their young root systems get badly shaken up when the trees are dug up at the nursery and they will not have the ability to go foraging for water. So, during their first summer in the garden, you must see that they do not go thirsty. As soon as dry weather sets in, they will want a good drink at least every three dry days. By a 'good drink' I mean not less than two gallons of water for each average-sized tree. Miniatures will not want so much, of course. Container-grown plants put in during the spring or summer months must be especially well treated, because they will tend to get thirsty very quickly indeed.

If you want to get young bushes flourishing quickly in your garden – and also if you want an extra special display from your established roses – try giving them some foliar feeds. This process is very simple and easy. Horticultural experts have discovered that many plants will absorb nutrients through the leaves as well as through the roots. So you simply drench the whole tree with a solution of a suitable feed once or twice a week during the months of May and June. Do not try to invent your own tonic mixture; use one of the proprietary liquid fertilisers specially formulated for the job and, again, stick strictly to the makers' instructions. The best time for drenching the trees is very early in the

(Top)
A rose bush is drenched with a foliar feed during May, using a watering can fitted with a fine rose. The same technique can be used to apply a systemic insecticide

(Bottom)
Foliar feeds can be applied using a diluter attached to the garden hose

morning, before the sun gets too strong. The second-best time is early in the evening when the sun is beginning to cool down, but you must do it soon enough for the leaves to dry off before dark. This is important, to avoid encouraging a premature attack of mildew. You can apply the feed with a garden syringe or, as I do, drench the trees using a watering can fitted with a fine rose.

If your garden has a very chalky alkaline soil and, despite the warning given earlier, you have 'taken a chance' and planted roses in the original ground, you may find your bushes developing a sickly pallor quite early in the season, with the leaves turning yellow between green veins. People with gardens on good soils may also find a few leaves turning yellow at the end of the summer, but they have no need to panic. It is when *all* the tree is looking poorly early in the season, and you know from your soil test that your ground is very alkaline, that you must do something about it. Buy a substance called Sequestrene and spray the roses with it or water it into the soil, as instructed on the pack. The object is to feed to the bushes, through their leaves, those essential nutrients which, because of the alkalinity of the soil, they cannot take up through their roots. I do not guarantee that the results will be perfect but it is the best method invented so far, and is the only corrective measure that is available to you.

coping with weeds

Until comparatively recent times, weeding a rose bed has involved a considerable expenditure of time and effort, either hacking away with a hoe or crawling around pulling the weeds out by hand. And in a rainy season when weeds flourish in wet ground, the job can be especially messy and unpleasant.

A mulch has a temporary smothering effect, but sooner or later, the weeds will appear through it.

Happily, though, horticultural scientists have come to the aid of gardeners with the introduction of two extremely useful and effective chemical weed controllers, called paraquat and simazine. Applied carefully and intelligently, they can be quite cheap to use. So let us examine the process by which they work and see how we can cope with the weed problem this easy modern way.

Paraquat is available to the general public from most garden shops under the brand name of Weedol. (This is the only brand available at the time of writing.) When dissolved in water and applied to the foliage of a living plant it is absorbed into the plant and kills it by inhibiting the photosynthesis process which is essential to plant life.

Simazine is sold as a rose-bed weed killer under several brand names; (be sure to buy the 'rose bed' not the very strong 'path' version of simazine). This also kills by inhibiting photosynthesis, but is taken into the plant through the roots. It is most effective against germinating weed seedlings. Simazine is a fine powder which, when well mixed with water and applied as instructed by the makers, settles in the top inch or two of soil and forms a toxic layer which remains effective for about six months. Once the weed killer is applied to the bed, the soil must not be disturbed or gaps will be created in the toxic layer, in which weed seeds may germinate and grow unharmed; neither can any new plant be placed in the bed during that six-month period. If you know that you will want to edge a rose bed with bedding plants for example, leave an untreated strip in which to put them. Simazine has the merit that, unlike sodium chlorate, another well-known weed killer, it does not spread to other parts of the garden where it is not wanted and is liable to damage plants – it stays precisely where you put it.

Roots lying below the toxic layer are unaffected – which is why the rose bushes are not killed – and so, if there are one or two deep-set roots of perennial weeds in the bed, these will grow up through it during the summer but no new weeds will appear.

From this you can see that there are two alternative techniques of weed killing you can use. One is to hoe out or kill off with paraquat all existing weeds in April, put down the fertiliser, followed by the mulch and finally, apply the simazine. The other is to put on the fertiliser and the mulch, wait a few weeks for the existing weeds to push through the mulch, and then apply the paraquat and the simazine together. If you decide to apply them together, make them up separately and combine them only just before application. The method of application I prefer is to use a plastic watering can fitted with a 'dribble bar'. You must be careful to apply simazine evenly over the bed so that one area is not made more or less toxic than the rest, as too strong a solution will harm the roses, and too weak an application will not be effective. But it is worth taking care to free yourself for six whole months from the drudgery of hoeing and hand weeding.

dealing with rose suckers

A rose tree is a rather remarkable piece of plant life which is not the single being made up of roots, shoots, leaves and flowers that it pretends to be. It is actually two different rose plants joined together. By a technique known as budding, the top part – the shoots, leaves and flowers – of one sort of rose is made to fuse with and grow upon the roots of another, usually referred to as a 'briar' or 'understock'. This arrangement is generally tolerated patiently by the understock, but just occasionally it gets rebellious about being denied a full and independent existence and throws up some shoots of its own which we call 'suckers'. If we allow these suckers to continue to grow, they will gradually absorb all the nourishment the roots can provide, and the top part, the rose you wish to grow, will starve to death.

So you will understand that you must learn to recognise a sucker growth when it appears and why you must remove it to save your tree from death by starvation. The difference between a young sucker growth and a desirable young shoot of the rose proper is difficult to describe in print – observation and experience are the best teachers. Certainly any shoot coming up from under the soil several inches away from the bush can be counted upon to be a sucker. But one that grows up among the shoots of the rose is more difficult to identify.

When you first start to grow roses, give every new shoot from the base of a bush rose the benefit of the doubt, and allow it to grow until it is a foot or so high. Then, the difference between a sucker and a genuine rose shoot will be much easier to spot. The sucker stem will be different in colour, and the leaves different in number, shape and texture, and probably, colour and size too. Look for these differences and, if possible, get an experienced rose grower to demonstrate them to you. A nursery is often a good place to get instruction: because of the huge quantities of plants being grown, there will usually be no trouble in finding such unwanted growth.

Having identified a sucker shoot, there is one way only to remove it, so that it will not grow again. Scrape the soil away carefully from the sucker and trace it to the point where it is growing from the understock, or find its roots and tear it right out so that nothing of the sucker shoot remains. Chopping the sucker off at ground level, or at any other point that is not its base, will only make matters worse, because dormant 'eyes' left below the point where you cut it will break into growth, and you will then have several suckers instead of just one.

On standard roses, anything growing from below that point at the top of the main stem where the real rose shoots emerge, is a sucker. Rip it off cleanly. Constant vigilance and prompt action on the lines suggested will ensure that sucker growth never becomes a problem.

(Top)
The difference between a sucker (right) and a desirable young shoot of the rose itself (left) must be learned by careful observation

(Bottom)
Tracing the sucker to the point where it is growing from the understock

(Top)
Ripping suckers from the main stem of a standard rose tree

(Bottom)
On a standard rose tree, suckers may appear anywhere up the main stem

CHAPTER NINE

fighting the insect pests

The number of different kinds of insects that could possibly come and suck, bite or chew the life out of your roses must run into hundreds. But please do not get perturbed because, in practice, very few of them will cause you concern. However, because of this large number, it would not be sensible to try to catalogue all of the pests for you. Instead, I will deal with the ones you are most likely to find on your roses, and group them according to the kind of damage they do, so that you can recognise them.

But, first, let us consider a few basic facts about pests in general. Every living thing in its natural environment has an enemy – something that hunts it down or lives on it parasitically until it destroys it. So, when we try to kill greenfly, for example, we are not alone. There are dozens of birds and insects that are also attacking it, although they may not destroy it quickly enough to suit us! Therefore, when we go into battle against an insect pest we want to do all we can to direct our fire accurately at the real enemy, and not spray insecticide around indiscriminately to kill friend and foe alike. An indiscriminate approach to spraying means that, having killed the insects who are our allies in the battle against greenfly we have to fight future generations of greenfly, all by ourselves. The future extermination of greenfly then will be more expensive, as well as having caused the death of harmless insects. Many of us have read about how the excessive use of DDT has 'backfired' on humanity, partly because some pests have developed an immunity to it and partly because, DDT being so indestructible, it has gone on killing useful friends long after it was first applied to kill insect enemies.

These considerations suggest three things. Firstly, do not always use the same insecticide against the same pest; (this will avoid the development of an immunity to the one insecticide by the particular pest). Secondly, do not use insecticides unnecessarily. It is waste of time and money spraying poisons around to kill a pest that may never come. Wait until the pest attacks your roses and then use an insecticide. Thirdly, avoid persistent insecticides that kill innocent friends long after the season of the original pest has passed.

If the number of possible pests is legion, the number of insecticides offered in the shops is almost as many. And, because of the many combinations of chemicals and different brand names, the whole thing is terribly confusing to the beginner who is only concerned that a pest is eating his roses and he wants to put a stop to it.

To put an end to the confusion, let me suggest that, if you are an absolute beginner, start with a basic kit of no more than two substances: a good brand of a systemic insecticide and one of liquid derris. A systemic insecticide is one that is absorbed into the sap stream of the plant and, for some weeks after, renders it poisonous to insects that suck it. Derris is a contact poison so you must hit the insect with it. It is non-persistent. Keep the spray away from fishponds because derris kills fish.

When you feel like going deeper into the subject of insecticides, there is a cheap little booklet called *Chemicals for the Gardener*, produced by the Ministry of Agriculture, Fisheries and Food and obtainable from H.M. Stationery Office or through booksellers. It is an excellent and 'easy-to-follow' guide to all the officially approved insecticides, the pests they will control and how to use them safely. It is revised frequently and each edition will keep you up to date with new products as they are approved.

Molly McGredy, a floribunda with hybrid tea-type flowers, won the President's International Trophy in 1968, as the best new seedling rose of the year

Now let us plan our pest control strategy. The one pest that most of us will meet every year is the sap-sucking greenfly. You cannot miss spotting greenfly on your roses, as it usually appears in large numbers on buds and young leaves quite early in the summer. When it appears, drench the trees with the systemic insecticide, following the manufacturers' instructions. A second dose, four to six weeks later, should keep your bushes clear of greenfly for the rest of the summer. You can put the insecticide on with a garden sprayer or drench the bushes using a watering can with a very fine rose. Use the systemic insecticide for two years, and in the third year change to a derris insecticide which, because it is non-persistent, will need to be applied more often. Put this on as a very fine mist with a garden sprayer.

Various sorts of bugs and caterpillars may nibble the flowers, bore into shoots or chew bits out of the leaves. As soon as you spot damage, go to work with the derris spray but aim it at the right target. If some flower buds are damaged, spray *all* the flower buds. If some leaves are chewed, spray *all* the leaves on all the rose bushes. Avoid spraying open flowers or you may kill visiting friendly bees. After two years add, for example, an insecticide containing BHC to your kit as an alternative to derris for these pests. By switching insecticides in this way you will prevent the various pests in your garden area developing an immunity to any one of them.

One pest that is difficult to deal with by spraying is a nasty maggot that rolls a leaf around itself, and goes on chewing away in its hiding place. This is called the rose leaf rolling sawfly. The best way to deal with this pest is the rather messy but effective method of pinching between finger and thumb any rolled or folded up leaves that you can spot on the bush and squashing the larvae that are hiding inside them.

(Top)
The one pest that is almost certain to visit every rose bed in the land – the sap-sucking aphid, commonly called greenfly

(Bottom)
One of the 'bugs' that attack the flowers is the thrip. This is the kind of damage that it does

(Top)
These rose leaves have been damaged by the rose leaf rolling sawfly

(Bottom)
There are many kinds of sprayer. This is the 'garden syringe' type of sprayer

(Top)
With this type of sprayer, the insecticide solution is carried around in the container on a back

(Bottom)
The rose slug worm eats both upper and under surfaces off the leaves. The worm and its damage to the undersides of the leaves is shown on the left, the upper-surface damage on the right

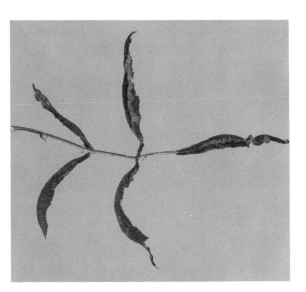

coping with diseases

Fortunately for the peace of mind of the beginner to rose growing, the rose is an exceptionally tough and, normally, healthy plant and, in Britain at least, is troubled by relatively few diseases or cankers.

Diseases tend to behave in a rather peculiar manner. They may appear during one summer and not another, so that the fact that a disease (other than rose rust) attacked this year does not necessarily mean that it will come again to plague you next year. This is just as well because, so far, horticultural scientists have failed to come up with any treatments which can actually kill off a rose disease once it has established itself on the bushes in your garden. All that science can offer are substances which you can use to protect your roses from contracting a disease during one season.

Having said that, let us go on to consider the troubles you may encounter and see what can be done to cope with them. Firstly, let us look at canker and die-back. During the early part of the season – that is, April, May and June – you may find one or two shoots displaying nasty-looking brown or black patches somewhere along their length: this is evidence of canker. By comparison with the healthy growth on the trees, these affected shoots stand out quite clearly as sickly and ailing. If these shoots are left unattended to, they will die anyway, but there is the danger that the infection could spread right down to the roots of the plant. So the obvious treatment is to cut off and burn the damaged shoots. When you do this, make your cut well below the affected area and just above an eye. Then look at the pith (the spongy tissue inside the shoot) of the part remaining and, if it is clear and white, you have removed all the damaged wood. But if the pith is stained brown, cut off some more of the shoot until you reach white pith. In an extreme case, you may have to remove an affected shoot completely.

In the case of die-back, shoots blacken and die from the tip downwards. Apply the same treatment as for canker, pruning out damaged shoots to an eye where the pith is clean and white. Infected shoots should be burned.

Incidentally, in some years recently, we have experienced warm spring weather which has encouraged new rose shoots to grow quite fast, and then a May frost has burned and blistered them and made the bushes appear very sickly. If this happens, do not panic, as the roses are not dead or diseased; just leave them as they are and let nature take care of them in her own time. In most cases, dormant subsidiary eyes will break into growth and take the place of the damaged shoots. Only if any of the stems start to die back later need you cut them down to fresh clean wood.

Now for other diseases: there are only three for you to worry about. These are mildew, black spot and rust. As I said earlier, there

(*Above*)
The cherry red hybrid tea rose Liebestraum has
very large and full flowers. The growth is vigorous
and upright. Trial Ground Certificate

(*Left*)
Josephine Bruce is one of the few roses with really
velvety-looking blooms. This hybrid tea rose is
very fragrant. It has a tendency to grow untidily,
and is liable to suffer from an attack of mildew.
Trial Ground Certificate

are no guaranteed cures, only preventives. Mostly, they are complicated chemical formulations which we need not consider in detail. It is wisest for the beginner to buy the product of one of the 'household name' firms for whichever of the diseases he wishes to combat.

Mildew we mentioned in chapter two as showing as a whitish coating which appears first on young leaves at the tops of shoots and, often, on the flower buds and stalks as well. It usually attacks from late July onwards, and seems to be more prevalent after a spell of damp and chilly nights. Some varieties are reasonably resistant to the disease and, if you grow only those varieties, you may never need to take preventive action against mildew. If you wish to protect other varieties, you can spray the young leaves with a mildew preventive, following the manufacturers' instructions, starting the moment you spot the first hint of trouble. As further new growth is made, that will need protection too, so you may need to repeat the spraying of your bushes about every ten days.

Black spot we also described in chapter two. It attacks roses growing in clean-air districts only, and then not every rose variety. It always starts on the oldest leaves nearest to the ground and gradually affects the upper leaves. Some modern floribundas and hybrid teas and, also, many of the rose species are reasonably resistant to it. If black spot is a serious

problem in your district, consider a course of protective spraying following the instructions of the maker of the product you choose.

Rose rust is, I believe, most likely to occur in the West Country but it has been known in other districts as well. Bright, rusty-looking spots appear first on the undersides of the leaves and, from there, the disease spreads. Rust can be a killer in some districts, so it is important to go into action with protective spraying immediately rust is observed. Also, it is wise to assume with this disease that, if rust attacked your roses last year, it will do so again next year. In this case you would, of course, start spraying in the second year *before* the disease put in an appearance.

(Top)
The blackened remains of a shoot killed by a severe May frost is held. But note how strong growths have come subsequently from the subsidiary eyes next to it

(Bottom)
Rose mildew distorts the foliage and covers it with a disfiguring dirty white powdery coating

(Top)
Rose mildew similarly attacks the flower buds as well as the leaves of roses

(Bottom)
Rose black spot disease is distinguished by the fringed and indeterminate edges to the spots

summertime attentions

Apart from the gardening chores of coping with such pests and diseases as may inflict their unwelcome presence on your bushes, summer should be a time for lazing, pottering and generally enjoying the beauty of your roses. One of those enjoyments is cutting a few blooms for the house and here is some advice to ensure that your cut flowers look really good. Many hybrid teas will produce one flower on a shoot, but there are some others that will produce small clusters of buds. For really fine cut flowers, reduce the clusters to a single bloom by pinching off the side buds as soon as they are big enough to handle, leaving the centre bud to flower. With the floribundas, one or two flowers in the truss will open first and the others will follow more or less together. In this case, if you try the reverse procedure and pinch out the few big buds, you will have a fine big truss with many flowers open at once to cut for the home.

The best times to cut roses are early in the morning or late in the evening. Select young flowers on which the outer petals are just opening and cut the stems just above a leaf joint. This is from where the next flowering shoot will develop. As you cut your blooms, put them straight into a container of deep tepid water – better still, use one of the modern cut flower preservatives – and leave them for a few hours in a cool place before putting them into an arrangement.

(*Opposite page, left*)
Orangeade is one of those floribunda roses that,
once you have seen it, you will always recognise
again by its brilliant colour, even from a distance.
Gold Medal

(*Opposite page, right*)
In good weather Papa Meilland, a strongly perfumed hybrid tea, can be very beautiful indeed,
but it really dislikes, and is easily spoiled by rain.
It is also liable to mildew

(*Below*)
Paddy McGredy has larger blooms than usual in a
floribunda rose. Gold Medal

(Top)
Some hybrid tea roses produce cluster of buds

(Bottom)
For really fine blooms, pinch out the side buds, leaving the centre bud to flower

Keep an eye on the garden display and, as the flowers fade and the petals fall, pick off the dead blooms to prevent the trees wasting their efforts trying to develop seed-pods. You will find, a couple of inches below the flower, a little- swelling on the stalk where the dead blooms can be snapped off quite naturally.

You may like to try your hand at growing some more bushes of your favourite varieties from cuttings. You can do this by rooting cuttings in pots in a greenhouse or on the kitchen window-sill, or alternatively, in some really good, fine soil in a warm and sunny spot in the garden. For a good cutting, wait until a nice strong shoot has flowered. Then before any side growths start to emerge, cut a section about 8–10 in. long from the middle of the shoot. Be careful to cut it so that there is an eye both at the top and the bottom of the section you are cutting. Remove from the cutting all except the top two sets of leaves, dip the bottom end into some hormone rooting powder (all garden shops sell it) and then plant. In the open ground, leave about a third of the cutting only showing above the soil, and if you have a sticky clay soil put some sharp sand (obtainable from a nursery) in the hole before planting the cutting. When growing it in a pot, you need not plant the cutting so deeply. In both cases keep the soil moist but not sodden.

Pot-grown cuttings will usually be ready for planting out in the garden the following June when all chance of a spring frost has passed. Open-ground cuttings must be left where they are, to grow on until the following autumn and then be carefully lifted and planted in their permanent place in the garden.

All rose enthusiasts should keep a record of the flowering behaviour of their varieties: the length of the flowering period, their reactions to bad weather and strong sunshine, their liability to black spot and so on. It can be revealing, and useful later.

(*Top*)
Dip the bottom end of a prepared cutting into hormone rooting powder before insertion

(*Bottom*)
A small trench is made with a spade in good soil in a clear sunny spot. If the soil is heavy clay, some fine sand is added to the bottom of the trench. The cuttings are inserted so that only one-third of their length is above soil level

(*Top*)
The trench is filled in and the soil is gently firmed around the cuttings. It is important that the soil is kept moist until a good root system has been established; this will generally take about one year from the time of planting

(*Bottom*)
Cuttings set in a warm and sunny spot in good soil are beginning to shoot during the following spring

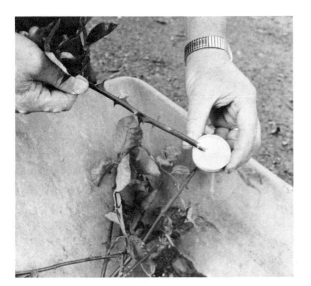

(Top left)
New Dawn is a rambler that has remained popular for forty years and could well do so for another forty. It can grow quite big if well fed

(Bottom left)
Orange Sensation is an excellent, bright and cheerful floribunda to grow where space is limited. Gold Medal

(Top)
Pascali is one of the best of the white hybrid tea roses, taking bad weather a little better than most roses of this colour. Certificate of Merit

(Below)
Peace is probably the most famous rose of modern times. With light pruning it can grow into an extremely large bush. It has plenty of healthy dark green foliage. Gold Medal

(Above)
Peer Gynt is a compact-growing hybrid tea rose. Certificate of Merit

(Below)
Piccadilly, one of the best scarlet and yellow bicolour hybrid tea roses. Certificate of Merit

(Top right)
Plentiful lives up to its name, giving masses of flowers on a quite small bush. It is a floribunda

(Right)
Princess Michiko is a strong, upright growing floribunda. Trial Ground Certificate

(Bottom right)
Queen Elizabeth comes second only to Iceberg in popularity among the floribunda roses. A very big and upright grower which makes a wonderful hedge, it is good for cutting and for showing. President's International Trophy

pruning established roses

Now we come to the last job in the rose year: pruning the established bushes in the garden. It is nothing like such a complicated and confusing job as it is often made out to be. So, if you are a beginner at rose growing, take heart for I intend to show you that pruning is a completely logical and simple process, really.

Although a rose is commonly referred to as a bush or tree, botanically it is a shrub. Each new shoot from this shrub grows, flowers, wears out and is replaced by further new shoots which grow up, all in the space of a few years. This means that an established rose bush in your garden will contain a mixture of young, adult and ageing shoots. The system of pruning we adopt is, therefore, aimed at encouraging the development of strong new growth and getting rid of old, weak and worn-out wood.

Before describing the pruning operation in detail, let us consider when it is best to do it. Over all of the southern and midland areas, you can prune at any time convenient time from November to March. In the north of England and in Scotland, it is customary to prune in March or early April.

Now, to illustrate the technique, let us trace the history of a bush rose shoot right through its life span; then you will be able to understand clearly why pruning is necessary and how it should be done.

A main basal shoot starts its life by growing up from around ground level during one summer and bearing a number of blooms. When these blooms have finished and the leaves have fallen it will look like the sketch in figure 1. The first pruning stage I am about to describe is the one usually carried out before planting new trees from the nursery, which I also described in Chapter 5, and also applies to basal shoots of established trees. Do this pruning by cutting off about half the shoot (figure 2) using sharp secateurs and taking care to make a clean cut a quarter-of-an-inch above an eye. Having made the cut, look at the pith of the part remaining and, if it shows a brown stain – which indicates that this part of the shoot is unhealthy – cut back further until you find clear white pith. Make this check on every pruning cut you execute – always.

During the second summer, new shoots, which we will call second-year growth, develop from the pruned basal shoot (figure 3). When you come to prune these, cut off about three-quarters of the second-year growth (figure 4).

In the third summer, further new shoots – the third-year growth – will come from the pruned second-year growths (figure 5). Prune these in similar fashion by cutting off about three-quarters of this third-year growth (figure 6).

You continue like this until that particular shoot structure starts to wear out and produces

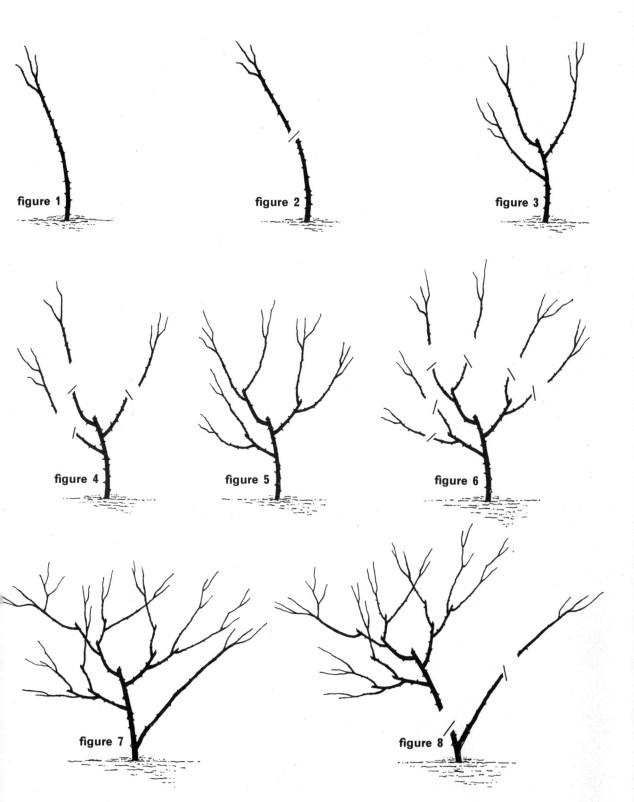

figure 1

figure 2

figure 3

figure 4

figure 5

figure 6

figure 7

figure 8

only miserable, twiggy growth. At this point you cut it right away to ground level.

Occasionally, you will find that a big, strong new shoot will break out from near the bottom of the original basal shoot (figure 7). When this happens, you get rid of the old growth by cutting it off just above the place from which this strong new shoot appeared and treat the newcomer as a basal shoot (figure 8).

Finally, from time to time you will find some thin, twiggy little growths appearing on a bush. Cut these off completely as they are of no value.

Now let us apply this approach to pruning an established bush in the garden. It will, if it has been well grown, have a mixture of shoots of all ages. Start by looking for new basal shoots and prune them as described in the first pruning stage. Next, start looking for second-year growths and prune them as described for this growth. Continue like this, pruning the different stages of growth that will be present on your established bush, as described above.

The point of cutting off a greater proportion of a second- or third-year growth than of a basal shoot is to try to ensure that, next summer, the resultant growths from all these pruned shoots will reach about the same height as the new basal shoots which will grow up amongst them. Thus we will have a nicely balanced bush with

(Left)
Shepherd's Delight can grow to be a big bush over four feet in height, but can contract black spot. Gold Medal

(Below)
Red Lion, a tall-growing hybrid tea rose, is becoming popular with those who like to try their hand at exhibiting. Trial Ground Certificate

(Right)
Ritter von Barmstede, one of the Kordesii climbers, is hardy and flowers freely

all the flowers showing up at about the same level on top of the bush.

You can apply the above pruning technique to all polyantha, floribunda and hybrid tea roses whether in bush or standard form. With the miniatures and with the species roses and their hybrids, you can, if you wish, leave them more or less to themselves and do hardly any pruning at all, apart from cutting away old shoots which have become worn out.

To prune climbers and ramblers, do not prune the strong new canes (shoots) coming from the ground or from low down on the tree. Instead, train these shoots in as they grow, tying them carefully to their supports. All other shoots on climbers you can cut back exactly as for bush roses.

Ramblers, if you have grown and fed them well, should make a sufficient number of long new basal shoots each year to enable you to cut out *all* those that have already flowered. Remember that ramblers grow new shoots in one summer that do not flower until the next. If a rambler does not grow sufficient new basal shoots to replace all those that have flowered, retain some of the best of the old ones but prune back by three-quarters of their length all the side shoots that carried flowers. Then start to feed the tree to encourage it to grow healthily again.

(Top)
The author commencing to prune a very big four-year-old bush of **Dorothy Peach**

(Bottom)
Applying the principles described in this chapter, the author is cutting back a strong second-year growth to the same height as the pruned basal shoots

(Top)
Here is the same **Dorothy Peach** with pruning completed; unpruned bushes of the same variety are in the background

(Bottom)
Sometimes strong basal shoots branch, as has occurred with this two-year-old **Stella**. The author is suggesting that the shoot should be cut down to the top eye below the branch

roses referred to in this book

There are many hundreds of varieties of the different classes of rose on the market today – far too many to name individually in a book of this kind. Those that are illustrated or are described in the lists which follow are representative of the classes concerned, but there is no reflection intended on any variety not included.

As a general guide to the probable satisfactory performance of a variety as a garden rose, the awards made by the Royal National Rose Society are good indicators. Most new introductions undergo a three year trial in the Society's gardens at St. Albans, at the end of which those that reach predetermined standards of achievement receive an award. There are four levels of award. Firstly, there is the Trial Ground Certificate (T.G.C.) which means that the variety should give a satisfactory performance in ordinary garden conditions. A higher standard of achievement is acknowledged by a Certificate of Merit (C. of M.), and a yet higher standard by a Gold Medal (G.M.). Provided that there is among them a variety of sufficient merit, the best of the Gold Medal winners of the year is awarded the President's International Trophy (Pres. Int. Trophy.).

MINIATURE ROSES

These little roses make bushes that range from 6–15 in. high in average conditions.

Baby Masquerade The flower buds are yellow and, as the flowers open, they gradually change to pink or red. The little flowers are semi-double, up to about 2 inches across when fully open. The foliage is medium green and glossy.

Colibre Bright orange-yellow double flowers, rather small in size, with a slight hint of fragrance. A very bushy little plant with glossy foliage.

Coralin The flowers are rather large for a miniature rose, ranging from coral to orange-red in colour. The foliage is plentiful, semi-glossy and light green in colour with some bronze tinting.

Perla d' Alcanada The colour is carmine red. Foliage is glossy and light green. This little rose is also known by the name Baby Crimson.

Pour Toi It has little semi-double flowers which are white with yellow tints at the base of the petals, and glossy medium-green foliage. You may also find this rose catalogued under three other names Para Ti, For You and Wendy.

Rosina This sunflower-yellow rose has a little fragrance at times. It grows rather bigger than most in the group. The foliage which is light green and glossy might be attacked by black spot in a bad season. You are very likely to find this variety listed as Josephine Wheatcroft and, occasionally, as Yellow Sweetheart.

(Top)
Stella displays an unusual and most attractive colour combination and produces blooms of sufficient size and quality to make it popular with those who like to enter for shows. Gold Medal

(Bottom)
Super Star is the most popular hybrid tea rose of the day. The light vermilion colour is unique and noteworthy for its purity. It grows rather tall. President's International Trophy

Scarlet Gem Rather large and full orange-scarlet flowers from which you may sometimes detect a little perfume. The foliage is substantial, dark green and glossy. This variety may also be catalogued as Scarlet Pimpernel.

Sweet Fairy An interesting lilac-pink colour with some fragrance. A quite low grower with matt, light green foliage.

DWARF POLYANTHA POMPONS

This group of dwarf growing, cluster roses contains varieties which grow from 1 to 2 ft. high and often spread as much or a little more.

Baby Faurax It is a most unusual violet-blue colour. The flowers are semi-double and are produced in large clusters, with glossy, light green foliage. There is some fragrance.

Cameo This has small, semi-double, salmon pink flowers, and has a reputation for being particularly free flowering.

Coral Cluster Rosette-shaped coral-pink flowers are borne freely in large clusters. This is a natural 'sport' from a rosy crimson variety called Orléans Rose and may 'revert': that is to say, some clusters of flowers may appear in the original colour and not the coral pink of Coral Cluster.

Ellen Poulsen These small deep pink flowers appear on what can be a very spreading bush. It has glossy light green foliage.

Miss Edith Cavell The flower is scarlet-crimson but the base of the petal shows white. It has small, dark green glossy foliage. You may find this variety listed under the names Edith Cavell or Nurse Cavell.

Paul Crampel This is a quite striking orange-scarlet colour which flowers freely. The foliage is leathery and glossy.

HYBRID TEA ROSES

The greater proportion of hybrid tea roses grow, in average conditions, to between 2 and 3 ft. in height. There are some, however, that normally grow smaller or very much larger

(Top)
The elegant shape, good fragrance and above-average growth of **Sutter's Gold**, together with glossy, dark green foliage make it a popular hybrid tea rose. **Certificate of Merit**

(Below)
Whiskey Mac is a hybrid tea rose of unusual colour although not, perhaps, of quite the classical form that most people associate with this class

(Bottom)
Wendy Cussons gives cerise blooms of very good form and pleasing fragrance. **President's International Trophy**

Where a variety illustrated or described below is markedly different in habit from the normal range – either in this or some other aspect – the fact is noted for your guidance.

Blue Moon Illustrated on page 15.

Buccaneer This is a very tall-growing buttercup yellow variety with a hint of fragrance. Trial Ground Certificate.

Champs Elysées The blooms are deep crimson of no exceptional form but good for garden display; a rather short grower.

Chicago Peace Illustrated on page 15.

Cleopatra This is a scarlet and yellow bicolour rose which flowers freely. It is a low-growing bush. The foliage is small and dark green. It may contract black spot. Gold Medal.

Colour Wonder This variety is an orange-salmon and yellow bicolour with rather small petals. There is a little fragrance, and the bush is low growing with glossy dark green foliage.

Diorama The apricot-yellow colour of this fragrant rose is very appealing. Trial Ground Certificate.

Doreen The bloom is orange-yellow with scarlet shading. There is some scent. The glossy dark green foliage may be attacked by black spot.

Dorothy Peach Illustrated on page 18.

Duke of Windsor Illustrated on page 19.

Ena Harkness Illustrated on page 19.

Ernest H. Morse Illustrated on page 19.

First Love A long, pointed bud opens to a pale pink flower. A free-flowering, tall-growing rose. Certificate of Merit.

Fragrant Cloud Illustrated on page 27.

Fritz Thiedemann This deep vermilion coloured shapely bloom has some fragrance. It grows as a bush of moderate to below average height. The variety flowers freely. Certificate of Merit.

Gail Borden The flowers are bicoloured rose pink and creamy yellow. The large blooms, which open quickly, are freely produced. It has attractive glossy green foliage. Gold Medal.

Gavotte In dry and mild weather this is a warm pink-shaded flower, large and beautifully formed, but it detests cold and wet. It grows very untidily, and may contract black spot. Certificate of Merit.

Golden Giant Illustrated on page 26.

Grand'mère Jenny Illustrated on page 27.

Grandpa Dickson Illustrated on page 26.

Isabel de Ortiz The flower is deep pink with a silvery sheen to the reverse side of the petal. The bush produces beautiful show blooms in warm weather but the petals wrinkle when it is cold; a tall grower. Gold Medal.

Josephine Bruce Illustrated on page 43.

King's Ransom Illustrated on the cover.

Lady Seton The blooms are a really beautiful and graceful deep rose-pink, and are long-lasting. It has good perfume. Certificate of Merit.

Liebestraum Illustrated on page 43.

Message A pure white rose of good shape which is quickly spoiled by rain and easily contracts mildew and black spot. Despite these weaknesses, it is popular for flower arranging.

Mischief The coral-salmon colour, good shape and strong fragrance of this rose have made it popular. It is a tall grower. President's International Trophy.

Miss Ireland The two-tone effect of this coral-salmon bloom with a lighter reverse makes it very attractive. It could be attacked by black spot. Certificate of Merit.

Mme Louis Laperrière This is a deep crimson, fragrant flower of no special form. It is generally below average height. Certificate of Merit.

Mojave This orange and reddish flame variety is popular for floral art. It is strong and upright growing with glossy, medium green foliage. Trial Ground Certificate.

Montezuma This is a hybrid tea which marks badly in cold rainy weather, but when the sun shines this massive grower produces armfuls of lovely deep salmon-red blooms. It is long-lasting in water which makes it an attractive choice for decorating the home. Gold Medal.

Papa Meilland   Illustrated on page 46.

Pascali   Illustrated on page 50.

Peace   Illustrated on page 50.

Peer Gynt   Illustrated on page 51.

Piccadilly   Illustrated on page 51.

Pink Favourite   This strong-growing, disease-resistant variety with deep rose-pink blooms has probably the loveliest foliage of any hybrid tea rose.

President Herbert Hoover   This rose has lovely shades of orange-gold and deep pink especially in the late summer and autumn, and has good fragrance. An extremely tall grower with exceptionally long flowering stems. The foliage is rather thin and prone to mildew.

Prima Ballerina   This deep pink rose freely offers a sweet perfume. It can be quite tall when well grown. Trial Ground Certificate.

Princess   This is a low-growing rose. It produces very large, full, vermilion flowers that hold their colour and resist rain remarkably well compared with other roses with so many petals.

Princess Paola   It has very sweetly-scented pink flowers, upright growth and matt, medium-green foliage. Trial Ground Certificate.

Red Devil   This does not care for cold wet weather, but given good conditions the blooms, scarlet with a lighter reverse, are big, beautiful and long-lasting. There is a good perfume and it makes a large bush. Certificate of Merit.

Rose Gaujard   The colour contrast of this elegant bloom – white flushed with pale pink, edged and veined carmine, with a silver reverse – shows best in warm sunny conditions. Even in bad weather though, this strong and disease-resistant rose does well in the garden. Gold Medal.

Royal Highness   Long, pointed, large and elegant blooms are soft, very pale pink. It has big, dark green foliage, and is very upright growing, a little above average height.

Santa Fé   This offers two tones of pink, the outer side of the petals being lighter in colour than the inner. Certificate of Merit.

Silver Lining   The inside of the petal is silvery rose, the reverse is nearly white. It has good form and fragrance. Gold Medal.

Stella   Illustrated on page 58.

Super Star   Illustrated on page 58.

Sutter's Gold   Illustrated on page 59.

Uncle Walter   This will grow to considerable height – as much as 6 ft. – with very little encouragement. Its flowers are scarlet with crimson shadings, full and slightly fragrant. Certificate of Merit.

Virgo   This is an elegant, long-pointed, white bloom, popular with flower arrangers but is not always a very strong plant. It is spoiled by rain and may get mildew. Gold Medal.

Wendy Cussons   Illustrated on page 59.

Wisbech Gold   This is a dwarf growing but bushy, golden yellow rose with a pink flush on the edges of the petals. It puts up with wet weather quite well, and has healthy mid-green foliage. Certificate of Merit.

Whiskey Mac   Illustrated on page 59.

Youki San   This is a white flower with some fragrance which may grow a little below average height. It is subject to mildew.

FLORIBUNDA ROSES

As in the case of the hybrid tea roses, most floribundas grow, in average conditions, to between 2 and 3 ft. high. Those with a tendency to be shorter or substantially taller are annotated to this effect in the captions to the illustrations and in the descriptions below.

Africa Star   It has moderately large flowers of lilac colouring; a low-growing variety with dark green foliage.

Alain   Glowing scarlet crimson flowers are borne in large trusses. The foliage is medium green in colour. Trial Ground Certificate.

Zéphirine Drouhin is over a century old but is still very popular. It has a pleasant perfume, and another attraction is that it has no thorns

Allgold   Illustrated on page 10.

Anna Wheatcroft   Illustrated on page 3.

Apricot Nectar   Illustrated on page 11.

Arthur Bell   Illustrated on page 11.

Athlone   This has cream flowers, each edged with orange-scarlet, which are slightly scented. It is a low grower with glossy foliage. Trial Ground Certificate.

Bobbie Lucas   Orange-salmon in colour, it is slightly below average in height but a reasonably upright grower: suitable for the small garden.

Cécile Brunner   Old enough to be classified as an 'old garden rose', this moderate to large bush carries trusses of perfect, elegant, miniature pale pink flowers.

Chanelle   Light peach pink, delicate blooms. It flowers freely and has some fragrance; dark green foliage. Certificate of Merit.

Charm of Paris   This rose has clear pink and well perfumed blooms. Its growth is of below average height. Certificate of Merit.

Chinatown   Illustrated on page 15.

City of Belfast   Illustrated on the cover.

City of Leeds   Illustrated on page 15.

Copper Pot   Illustrated on page 18.

Daily Sketch   This is a tall-growing bush with dark green, glossy foliage. The Blooms, which are large for a floribunda, are reddish-pink with a silver reverse. Gold Medal.

Dearest   This is a rose that does not like wet weather, but when the climate is dry and mild the rosy-salmon flowers look very beautiful. Gold Medal.

Dorothy Wheatcroft   Illustrated on page 18.

Elizabeth of Glamis   Illustrated on page 19.

Escapade   This makes a low-growing bush which shows off the blooms' rare colouring – lilac-rose, paling to white in the centre. They are quite large and semi-double. Certificate of Merit.

Europeana   The rosette-shaped, deep crimson blooms are like one of its parents, Rosemary Rose. It tends to sprawl and is liable to get mildew. Certificate of Merit.

Evelyn Fison   Illustrated on page 23.

Frensham   This rose has semi-double deep scarlet crimson flowers in large trusses. A very tall and branching grower, it makes a big splash of colour. It is liable to get mildew. Gold Medal.

Gallant   Illustrated on page 27.

Goldgleam   Illustrated on page 22.

Golden Slippers   This has bicolour flowers, orange-flame inside, yellow outside. The colours fade rather quickly. It is a low grower with glossy, medium green foliage.

Gold Marie   The blooms are golden yellow, stained with crimson in bud; slightly fragrant flowers. This is a strong grower with glossy foliage which seems to resist disease very well.

Iceberg   Illustrated on page 30.

Irish Mist   Illustrated on page 35.

Jan Spek   This has a low-growing habit very suited to small gardens. The yellow colour fades to cream as the flower ages. Trial Ground Certificate.

Korona   This is a very free-flowering orange-scarlet variety. Above average height, it is upright in habit and very thorny. It might get black spot. Gold Medal.

Lilli Marlene   Scarlet-red, semi-double, long lasting blooms. Flowers freely on below average height bushes. Certificate of Merit.

Lucky Charm   This has strongly scented golden-yellow and flame-coloured flowers which are quite large. There is dark green glossy foliage, with some bronze tints; the rose can get black spot.

Marlena   This rose is a dwarf grower with bright red, cupped flowers freely produced; it is good for small gardens.

Molly McGredy   Illustrated on page 39.

Orangeade   Illustrated on page 46.

Orange Sensation   Illustrated on page 50.

Paddy McGredy   Illustrated on page 47.

Paprika   A very striking turkey red colour, the semi-double, large flowers are freely offered; dark green glossy foliage. Gold Medal.

Pink Parfait   The pink flowers with yellow at the base are an attractive hybrid tea shape and quite large. A slightly above average height, strong-growing bush, it has plenty of semi-glossy foliage. Gold Medal.

Plentiful   Illustrated on page 51.

Princess Michiko   Illustrated on page 51.

Queen Elizabeth   Illustrated on page 51.

Red Dandy   The classical 'hybrid tea' shaped flowers are a bright scarlet-crimson. The bush is tall-growing with matt, medium green foliage. Certificate of Merit.

Red Favourite   This is a fairly low-growing variety with semi-double crimson-scarlet blooms freely produced. It has medium green, glossy foliage. Certificate of Merit.

Rosemary Rose   This is very popular with flower arrangers. The bright carmine colour and the rosette shape seem just right for each other. It may get mildew. Gold Medal.

Sarabande   This is an extremely eye-catching low-growing bedding rose, with bright scarlet flowers.

Scarlet Queen Elizabeth   Orange-scarlet blooms, this grows very tall like the floribunda parent from which it is named. Trial Ground Certificate.

Scented Air   This is well named – for a floribunda rose it is exceptionally fragrant. The flowers are salmon-pink and moderately full. Certificate of Merit.

Shepherd's Delight   Illustrated on page 54.

Zambra   The rather small semi-double flowers are orange on the inside of the petal, yellow on the outside. It is slightly below average height, and may get black spot on its glossy foliage. Certificate of Merit.

SHRUB ROSES

The various kinds of shrub roses embrace a wide range of habit of growth and size of bush. Those listed here can usually be relied upon to reach five feet in height, but when well grown, may attain the greater heights indicated in the descriptions.

Bonn This is a free-flowering, musk-scented variety with orange-scarlet flowers. It can grow up to 7 ft. tall, with large, light green foliage. Certificate of Merit.

Fred Loads Illustrated on page 23.

Heidelberg Large, bright red flowers are produced on a big spreading bush, which could grow to about 6 ft. tall. Certificate of Merit.

Kassel This has scarlet-red fragrant flowers on a bushy plant, which can reach 6 ft. in height. Certificate of Merit.

Lady Sonia There are deep golden-yellow flowers, which are quite large. This makes a big thick shrub which can grow to about 7 ft. in height, with glossy, dark green foliage. Certificate of Merit.

CLIMBING ROSES

The climbers in this list, with the exception of those for which a special note is given, are of average size – a spread of 6 to 10 ft.

Albertine Illustrated on page 10.

Altissimo This rose is a compelling deep red, with single flowers on a good strong plant. It has matt, medium green foliage. Certificate of Merit.

Casino Illustrated on page 14.

Copenhagen The large, fragrant, scarlet blooms have good form, and are freely produced. It has glossy foliage. Certificate of Merit.

Danse du Feu Illustrated on page 18.

Dortmund The very attractive single flowers, red with a white centre, are freely offered. It has glossy, medium green foliage, and can grow to above average size.

Golden Showers Illustrated on page 22.

Hamburger Phoenix See illustration on page 35.

Handel This has cream coloured blooms with a pink flush on the edges of the petals, together with dark green foliage. Trial Ground Certificate.

New Dawn Illustrated on page 50.

Parkdirektor Riggers The semi-double flowers are blood red and freely produced, with glossy dark green foliage.

Pink Perpetue The blooms are clear pink inside, carmine pink outside. It is a free flowering variety which will not spread too far, dark green foliage. Certificate of Merit.

Ritter von Barmstede See illustration on page 55.

Royal Gold This rose has fragrant, deep yellow flowers with moderate growth and medium green foliage. It may be cut back by frost in a severe winter.

Zéphirine Drouhin Illustrated on page 62.

Acknowledgements

The author gratefully acknowledges the help received from the following in illustrating this book: *Amateur Gardening*, Robert J. Corbin, Ernest Crowson of J. E. Downward, Valerie Finnis, C. Gregory and Son Ltd, R. Harkness and Co. Ltd, May and Baker Group of Companies, S. McGredy and Son Ltd, Elsa M. Megson, Murphy Chemical Co. Ltd, Harry Smith and Wheatcroft Brothers Ltd.